Terrain

Dan Bellm
Molly Fisk
Forrest Hamer

Hip Pocket Press
Nevada City, California

Copyright © 1998 by Dan Bellm, Molly Fisk, Forrest Hamer
All rights reserved

HIP POCKET PRESS
520 Nursery St.
Nevada City, CA 95959

We gratefully acknowledge the publications in which some of these poems first appeared:

Beloit Poetry Journal: "The calling."
Charlotte Poetry Review: "Celestial navigation."
Estero: "Explanation."
Manoa: "The last hour of the night."
Mudlark: "Hunter's moon," "Nauset."
Ploughshares: "Brightness."
Poetry: "Before words," "Silence."
Poetry Flash: "True story."
River Styx: "Boy wearing a dress."
33 Review: "Invitation."
TriQuarterly: "Illinois River."
Wild Duck Review: "Jupiter."
Yalobusha Review: "Arrival, the city of Bethames," "Couples," "Siren song."
ZYZZYVA: "Getting happy," "Moving on," "The names of streets," "Surface tension."

"The calling" and "Getting happy" also appeared in *Call & Response* by Forrest Hamer (Farmington, Maine: Alice James Books, 1995). "Getting happy" was reprinted in *The Best American Poetry 1994*, edited by A.R. Ammons and David Lehman (New York: Scribner, 1994) and in *Strange Attraction*, edited by Howard Junker (Reno: University of Nevada Press, 1995). "Explanation" also appeared in *Salt Water Poems* by Molly Fisk (Fairfax, CA: Jungle Garden Press, 1994), and was reprinted in *Wild Duck Review*. "On the disinclination to scream" first appeared in *Sexual Harrassment: Women Speak Out* (Freedom, CA: The Crossing Press, 1992), and was reprinted in *Onthebus*, *The Healing Woman*, and *Resource Woman*. "The Dry Tortugas" was featured as first-place winner in *The Denny Poems 1995-1996*, the Billee Murray Denny Poetry Anthology (Lincoln, IL: Lincoln College, 1996). "Angkor Wat" was featured in the *Emily Dickinson Award Anthology* (Williams, AZ: Universities West Press, 1998). "Lament" and "Before words" were set to music by the composer Jorge Martín, as part of a sequence entitled "Of Fathers and Sons" (1997). "Boy wearing a dress" was reprinted in the *San Francisco Bay Guardian*. The title "the names of streets instead of streets..." is taken from the poem "Delle Avenue," by Dan Bellm.

We would also like to thank the Squaw Valley Community of Writers, which first brought us together, and the teachers and friends who have helped us along the way.

ISBN 0-917658-30-2

Designed by Elaine Joe
Oak tree design by Carl Dern
The text of this book is set in Weiss.

Contents

5	Testimony
6	Before words
8	Celestial navigation
9	Silence
11	Origins
12	Explanation
13	Siren song
16	Shore
17	First winter
19	Artaud, etcetera
21	Hanapepe
23	Emerging, specific
25	Couples
26	Nauset
27	Brightness
29	A month of Sundays
30	Jupiter
32	9 poems
33	Incarnate
34	Kindling

35	True story
36	Gardener
38	Angkor Wat
39	Lament
40	On the disinclination to scream
42	Invitation
43	The language
45	The peacemaker
46	Prayer for Joe's Taco Lounge, Mill Valley
48	The last hour of the night
50	The calling
55	Illinois River
59	"the names of streets instead of streets..."
60	Moving on
63	Hunter's moon
64	Arrival, the city of Bethames
65	Nashvillanelle
66	Surface tension
67	Getting happy
69	Boy wearing a dress
71	The Dry Tortugas

Forrest Hamer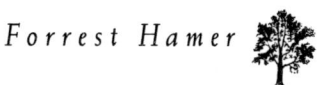

Testimony

    Now, and then, I regret the years I lived without
              poetry, not writing toward it,
the years not only before, when I was
              a child, but later, when I then knew
    writing and left it anyway, because
              I was afraid, because I had nothing
      yet to say. It's like the way
my mother talked of her years without God, the service
              and its blessings ever lost. But God, ever
    patient, wondering when she'd come to find herself
              what she'd have to say.

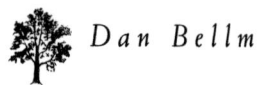 Dan Bellm

Before words

A baby is singing in the morning
before anyone is up in the house

Before he has decided
which of all the languages he will speak
he is trying the sounds of his voice
in the first light

He hears a man
come up the street collecting bottles
just ahead of the garbage truck
straining uphill
to come throw them away

He hears the shriek of glass
It is like the vessels of Creation
breaking in God's hands

He hears the wind around the house
and in the wind
every word he will ever say
and what will stay unsaid

Dan Bellm

and stops to listen to silence
and sings to it
the way the body addresses the soul
lending it shape

lending it comfort and sorrow

The body wants to be useful
and the soul is open so wide

This is the way we awaken
He remembers he is alone
and cries for us.

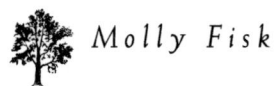 Molly Fisk

Celestial navigation

Through the mouth of the Golden Gate
they slip in ones and twos,
and the morning sun lifts
over the last ridge and blesses them
with her pink light. They glide
along the horizon to a point
at the center of my open window
and turn. Some angle south,
their massive sterns still brightly lit,
making for San Diego, Ecuador.
The others swing toward me—as toys
on a flat blue summer lake
are cheered by a boy on the shore,
I clap for them and point them west: Hawaii,
Hong Kong, Japan. I will not live forever.
May never learn what each one carries.
Cars. Rice. The sweet fruits of this earth
we bow and offer to one another.
Who will guard them when I'm gone?
They seem to come from another time—
so huge and slow; old as whales—the ancient
and outdated shapes neglected, almost useless,
now that most of life wings through the air
at lightning speed, bouncing
off the metal stars we've hung above us.

Dan Bellm

Silence

in memoriam John Cage

Just a few lights on at the camp across the lake—
    no boats—no voices—no birds—no wind—
        and nothing but light reaches us this far
from the deafening stars which aren't even there
        any more—it's a silence we never know
    in the city but there's still the sound of the mountain
        falling and the valley rising up,
    the sound of the heart and breath,
the sound of thought travelling from nowhere
        to the roar inside the ear—
    there is no such thing as silence—
which at least is what the dead
        composer used to say but what would he say now?
Tonight we are mad at each other and everyone and selfish
        and want to be left alone
    but there is no such thing as alone,
        and though we want to be on vacation
from whatever it is we do when we are not on vacation
    there is no such thing as a vacation—
        the baby wakes up
    at 1 and 2 and 5 a.m.
because his body can't stop moving all night
    because it's growing, because he's learning to walk,

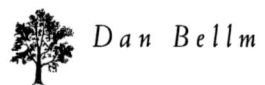 Dan Bellm

>   because he has nothing to get away and rest from
>   and there is no such thing as rest—
>   this morning when he took six seven eight steps
>   across the kitchen and sat down
> plop and clapped his hands like wingbeats
>   of a bandtailed pigeon taking off over
>   treetops his happiness made us both
> happy a moment—we had been sitting
>   miserably peacefully furious in the silence
>   between one wave clapping at the dock and the next—
>   there is no such thing as silence—

Forrest Hamer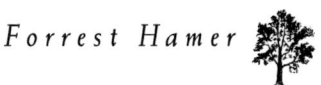

Origins

Thinking he was asking about race, I told him I was black;
and, thinking he was asking where I come from, I told him
I was from the South and from here in California and, really,
I am from the people I love who love me; and, thinking
he was asking about my sexual orientation, I told him, yes,
I am sexually oriented, especially with some men; then,
thinking he was asking about my religion, I told him I had none
to speak of save for my awe of the spirit; and, hearing
him ask specifically where I was coming from, I told him then
I come from wherever it is strangers tell their lives
in ways far less specific than speaking to each other dreams,
which is how, if I had been thinking, I should have told him
about myself.

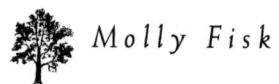 *Molly Fisk*

Explanation

Finally I just gave up and became an animal.
I slept when I was tired,
sometimes dropping in mid-stride,
curling into a knot on the sunny floor.
I ate raw food at odd hours,
wiped my mouth on the back of my hand,
stopped brushing my hair.
The phone rang, but I didn't answer it.
Mail lay unopened on the stairs. Flowers
drooped in dry pots. Dust sifted down
from the ceiling in hazy swirls.
I left the windows open.
After a few weeks I grew
accustomed to it, sank deeper
into my actual body, learned to love
the hours as they passed.
I let go of the spinning
human world and walked in the hills at night
under a changing moon.
Deer swung their heads toward me.
I sat beside them in their beds of creaking grass
listening to crickets ticking in the heat.
I cooled my skin in the ocean, licked
the crusted salt from my arms.
In time, my throat forgot to speak,
it lost the bright angles of consonants,
the dark sloping vowels. It joined the chorus
of mute life with a kind of hum.

Dan Bellm

Siren song

The older hikers are staring into the water —
it looks too hard to get down to it over the rocks —

and the woman tells her husband, it's all right,
she's close enough, she's seen enough,

but she doesn't sound convinced and he knows it, turning away —
he's tired now, but she would like to go further, as I

am going, because I still have strong legs and good boots
she envies, I suppose, almost lured to try, and then

they are gone. It takes me only a minute to clamber down
and ford the swampy inlet, wet to the waist,

and I'm swimming to the raised tip of the dead limb
at the center of Shirley Lake like one preserved past age

in the delicious chill that calls to mind
how geniuses are having their brains frozen now

against a future they trust will remember them
and sigh for their return, but what if

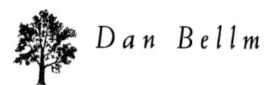 *Dan Bellm*

your brain isn't your best feature
or your noblest part, as if even the noblest skull-mass

isn't past useful freeze-drying at the point of death,
shocked too often by blips of logic or passion,

too many of its little brilliancies lost in corridors
like books misfiled in the library and therefore lost,

simply not there? So I wish my legs to be iced up instead
for striding and climbing through as much of time as I am able,

walking ahead of others as I have always left my companions
irritably lagging a yard or so behind

but haven't the bones shifted place themselves
under the sedimentary loosening sway of the spine

and the muscles come unmoored enough under the pubic bone
to make my youth unreturnable to me even in the age

when the cryogenic dead shall be raised incorruptible?
And this is why a pain shot down the leg this morning

as soon as the hiking boot went on, the sorry limb
knew it was being summoned for another test of greatness

Dan Bellm

and thought about failing graciously with a small thank-you,
staying to recline in the hotel lobby in the valley

stroked by the coffinlike plush of the sofas,
guessing at how it will be to stir inside the box for centuries

whenever the earth contracts and settles
under the compacting entrance of more and more death,

its weakest joint, the sprained V
of its gone sexual exuberance, numbing slightly

at the arrivals of beings it cannot shift or turn to nestle against
because there is always more numbing,

more separation into ever finer dust,
a decomposition as patient as this granite's into the meadow

as I swim back seriously shivering now
to sun myself, naked as a siren on the rock,

one of the immortal beauties, a warning, a temptation,
combing my silvering hair.

 Forrest Hamer

Shore

One day, by the stark water, you notice
how many old there are still alive, none of them your mother
only one of them your father who doesn't remember

how to find his way to church or sometimes
back home from the store; and you notice
there are just as many younger than you, and you wonder

where are the people like you in the middle,
and what else can they see; and all of this is to say
you've had a dream your parents were still alive,

the age you are now,
and they were flirting with each other, playful
in the small boat setting out away

from the dock you were standing on, you
watching her sink back into him, watching them happy,
feeling happy once more yourself, living nearly

the middle of happiness; and there is this feeling
you'd been flirting with that might last,
even if you forget ever dreaming about it.

Molly Fisk

First winter

A cold night, the power out, and February,
where they are slowly chipping calico
layers of wallpaper off a kitchen ceiling,
balanced on wooden ladders they dragged
from under a tarp in the barn. Votives on the counter,
and in the next room their first necessary fire.
She has already taught him to make cinnamon
toast, leave room for the milk in her tea.
He has taught her he won't leave.
Together, they have painted the living room
black-eyed Susan yellow, planted lilacs.
They don't know how hard it will be.
The first layer of paper's crisp black and red
is as painful, in the old house, as the place
where the scraper slices his palm. Blood
wells to match the ceiling, a few bright
drops splash, almost lost on the spattered
linoleum floor. She hunts up a bandaid,
abandoned in the medicine chest, and wipes the cut
clean with an old towel. They have made their vows.
Candlelight spins the shadows of their hands
across rain-slick window glass. They scrape
until their shoulders ache, through decades
of wall paper, past all their previous lovers,

Molly Fisk

the college blue books, diaphragms and operettas,
past the damp palms of high school dances,
the caught frogs and molding petri dishes of third
grade, to the smiles of their exhausted mothers
on the different days they were born,
each successive layer softer-toned and sweeter
than the last, until they reach gold roses
on pale green stems, and stop to admire them.

Molly Fisk

Artaud, etcetera

I decided to marry him the day he reached for my hand in front of two of his friends without stopping in the middle of a sentence. He was talking about French surrealists and I was sitting on the floor—he was in one of those awful wicker chairs in the living room of his parents' second, slightly less wonderful, ski house, my shoulder beside his knee. His friends were also writers, we were at a summer camp for writers, but they were real friends, the kind that want to talk about themselves not quite as much as they want to listen to him.

Later, when I knew him better and had been crying perhaps, or was tired after a long day, I would rest my cheek against his jeaned thigh and he'd catch my hair up between his knuckles, but this was the first day we'd been quote-unquote together, we had made love in his bedroom downstairs, unexpectedly (by which I mean that I was hoping something was happening but had just got the idea to investigate, and stopped by his house, and then, boom!—and then we snuck down to the Red Dog where he had a beer, against his mother's wishes. He was 46 then, but a head injury had made him susceptible as a kid

Molly Fisk

to the desire to rebel, and first fucking someone in the afternoon, not just any someone, but me, and then drinking a dark draft on the deck of the Red Dog was exactly what the doctor ordered), and this was the test: any other man I knew would soon be starting the long chill, sending me shorter smiles, leaning almost imperceptibly away, and occasionally, although it's a cliche now, checking his watch, while this man, voice like a trombone and mouth full of Dali and Jarry and absinthe, reached across his own knee and took my hand.

Dan Bellm

Hanapepe

Curled warm at my back asleep you wake me
crying softly in my ear
in the dark. Low clouds whirling
over the mountain. Hard rain all night
swallowed up in red earth.
Harvest time, fields burnt clean,
trucks up and down the rutted road
with loads of gnarled cane
stacked high. Sweet odor
of manured sugar plowed under.
We are alone
in the middle of the ocean
visited far from home by the dead
we have buried. So many:
they have come over the water
to remind us
in our sleep. Breath of ghosts
in the four-petalled flowers. Ghosts
in the cane. A plume of sweet smoke
from the mill stack.
Names on scraps of paper
burning. Smoke of words in dreams.
Married, bound to each other,
we have greened and prospered, two men

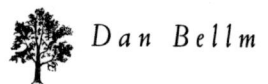 *Dan Bellm*

sorrowful over joy.
When I whisper your name you scream
that people are dying. We must be dying too.
I whisper to wake you
and you scream for light.
Hard rain all night
swallowed up in red earth.

Forrest Hamer

Emerging, specific

Almost. He almost had her; but,
filled with his ecstasy of almost　　　(*all and most*)
having her again, Orpheus looked

back.
Not content to animate the dead
world, not content with knowing,　　　(*and with knowing he had done nothing*
　　　　　　　　　　　　　　　　　　　　at first, had done nothing
　　　　　　　　　　　　　　　　　　　　that first time—)
he looked again and lost her.
Once more and (now) for ever.
Just his luck:

In a song he sings about rain, the gods weep for their children
but only when it is time to weep over foolishness.
After this season passes, the gods return to encouraging desire.

　　　　　: she has forgotten him.

　　　　　: when she has come above the underearth, he sees each time
　　　　　 she is not the one he has gone looking for.
　　　　　　The truth is : : there is no one he has gone looking for.

 Forrest Hamer

What, then is his sight?

One moved to him by raining?
She who bore him deeply?
He who would lie with him?

(And his loss?)

He thinks. He supposes. He assumes.

Molly Fisk

Couples

Hold on to what you remember,
this exact summer, everything unchanged,
the blue Ford Falcon with its handle-crank
back window rolled down driving
the green length of Argilla Road,
all the cousins under ten then,
eight of us crammed into the way-back
singing Day Tripper, singing Can't Buy Me Love.
We are salted and sandy, shreds of brown kelp
still caught in our bathing suits,
the melting ice cream cones already
thrown out the window; we are baked;
we are quarreling and happy.

The desultory remarks of four tired parents
float over our heads and into that summer:
they are thinking of gin, and tonic,
and four o'clock volleyball, getting the kids
washed, shucking the corn and feeding them,
do we have enough hot dog buns, stopping
at Aggie's for another pack of cigarettes.
The muscular fathers, up in the front seat,
are trading old jokes and both looking forward
to the low-backed sleeveless cotton dresses
of the other men's wives and our mothers know it,
but nothing is wrong yet, everyone's cheerful.

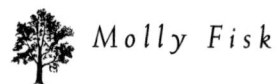 Molly Fisk

Nauset

When my grandmother said Act like a post,
I slid down to my knees and held completely still.
We watched the gull chicks gradually relax
and lift out of their camouflage in footprints
and tire tracks. As soon as they ran she'd be up
to throw her shadow over them, tripping a little
in the loose sand, and where they froze again
at the predator I fixed my eyes so I could direct her.
Rafts of ducks floated on the swell outside the breakers,
least terns screamed overhead, and the whole
colony of gulls dive-bombed us. She carried
the scar of one's bill along the length
of her part, which was why we wore hats.
I carry the high shriek of gulls into sleep
years later, sand still in everything, the blue glare
squinting my eyes while her voice says
Hold him gently, and she slips the silver band
around a yellow leg, her gnarled, meticulous hand
working the pliers to twist it shut and the heat
still rising and the surf banging.

Dan Bellm

Brightness

Driving home from the hospice, from his death,
4 a.m. now, his last possessions in a paper bag
beside me on the seat, the heavy glasses,
the teeth in a margarine tub,
his cheap watch on my arm as though I'd stolen
time back, the smell of his skin
on my hands; over the city
where I was born there's a sliver
of glass, the new moon
with the old moon in its arms;
so dark, and no one on the streets
as if this were my dream city
that I won't have to share with anyone,
enclosed apart in its own time
but a little changed, a little decayed
from the way I remember it, separate
from me after all, going its own way; it is not
my memory; time has not stopped; my father is dead.
O ferocious soul with your famous mistrust of love,
I think your darkness
must be my inheritance;
I reach the edge of the city, drive west on Highway 36
and there is no one under the shelter of darkness
but me and two or three truckers on the road,

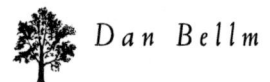 Dan Bellm

early risers like you, starting the working day
before anyone else has stirred; so the far past
returns and you come into my room softly
to tap me out of sleep
in the dark, we go for a ride in the truck
somewhere, you and me, shivering awake, our breath visible,
alone in our bodies,
alone in the world.

Forrest Hamer

A month of Sundays

The first Sunday after the Sunday you were buried,
we talked for almost forever, walking together
toward home, in the middle of a long road.

The next Sunday after, we'd fought, and I had to return
to California, and we were saying goodbye, saying
people who love each sometimes get on
each other's nerves, and these are small matters.
We held each other for the long time
we held each other when I left last summer.

The third Sunday after, I woke up not having dreamt,
wanting to call home, knowing Dad would be at church
and the answering machine would pick up, your voice clear
as dream, promising you would call me back.

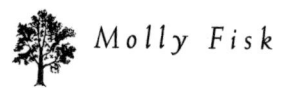 Molly Fisk

Jupiter

I wake up at four with the bright white beads of a headache
strung behind my eyes, shifting and clicking, an abacus

counting out sorrows. Click. I am alone. Click. I haven't
had children yet. Will anyone know me or love me?

Regret. All morning I count change into the outstretched
hands of strangers as if I were spilling the letters of my name

into their open palms. Expecting a flicker of recognition.
I bag their maps and books—give half a smile, directions.

I wonder when my life will turn out. Where's the assurance
we had as kids, when things made sense and dinnertime

always came at dusk, a call from the porch, pale globes
of whiffle balls glowing like moons at the lawn's shadowy edge.

                                          Outside the windows
it's black, and cool for August. Sagittarius chases the scorpion

slowly across the southern sky. In Latin the word for planet
is wanderer: Jupiter pulls at the end of his orbit, invisibly

Molly Fisk

leashed to the sun, but from here it looks like he's weaving,
drunk, among the mythical pictures—Hunter, Bears, Dog,

Virgin—drawn by people already centuries dead.
Night after night I watch him roam, and in every American town

there are others, lying flat-backed in wheatfields and ballparks,
empty lots, or leaning against a window like this, with a glass

still half-full of water, aspirin swallowed,
foreheads pressed to the dark.

 *Dan Bellm*

9 poems

Nothing but horizon, Dad, laid bare by pioneers like you

◆

Cardiologist so happy: as you die she restarts your heart

◆

a rift, a fault, a break in relation-
      ship, an opening, an open space

◆

Funeral flowers: two sisters still not speaking

◆

Solace, worst enemy, mirror ghost father

◆

Feel a certain power over you dead I don't want—

◆

uphill road, old green Ford: creeper vines around the wheel

◆

it's here somewhere it's only lost

◆

"Go to sleep it's late" "No it's not late any more"

Forrest Hamer

Incarnate

There are just too many of them, the dead too many to be

this way they are, crowding a realm other than here,

my mother among them, since the beginning the soul made many,

continuous, what of when we die, this way we are, where

could there be place enough for us, soul so full.

for Jean Valentine

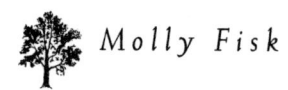 *Molly Fisk*

Kindling

for Robert Frost

I watched you with those dry stone walls, the fitting and shifting,
using gravity, shape and no mortar, sweating, splitting the meaning

finer and finer, as if it were kindling. I learned about work
from following your obstinate tracks on the page.

My family gave me your general terrain: the late September aster,
brooks, birches, moon of standing water shining back at me

from ruts in the Dowsville Road. But you gave me the stated pain,
the thing said, found the smile inside your loneliness and wore it.

No one else cried Reluctance and Acceptance in the same breath,
or talked to smoke, cracked subtle jokes at God's expense.

How I loved your old clothes, woven of ambition and patience,
and the idea of Job's wife's disgust, backlit by her husband's earnestness.

My respect is partly inherited, although I doubt you'd recognize
my mother, the acolyte, so happy you had dipped one foot in the Pacific

that she cried, reluctant emigre to California, reading your poems aloud,
over and over, trying to herd all her children into sleep.

Dan Bellm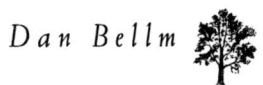

True story

for Bo

Darling you should contract a terminal illness he'd say
you're writing too slowly and give that Tallulah smirk,

waving a bony arm at me and flicking ash: four books
in three years, each one a lifetime past the one before,

while the virus stole his body from his mind. I could only
watch him burn, the way he'd sit and roll a clean

page into the machine and type Chapter 1 Page 1 and pull
the most demented stories out his head from start to finish

in the proper order, each one a lifetime truer than the one
before. Now he comes to me from death in the middle of

the night as a live coal in my heart, a pang that wakes me up:
he says *Darling you want pain?* I want to turn a light on

to get hold of myself but close my eyes to stay in the dark.
He says *All right. I'll give you pain.* He says *Someday*

it just might kill you. If it's any comfort. Someday soon.

 Forrest Hamer

Gardener

After Sundays pass, you stop tending
the way your life just rushes through
what happens next and next and next.
In the meantime, hairs the color of ashes
sprout from your head like sprigs of bush
your mother sent last winter.
You decided against planting,
thought yourself too busy and unlucky
to grow again the lawn from home
these years and miles away;
but you've been guessing at the names of flowers
in yards you pass on the way to work,
and will now imagine bougainvillea
climbing the wall of your porch.
Maybe gray hair has been there all along,
underneath, but times itself to come out now,
now when you need to be startled
so you notice how fast your life is going,
how filled it is with work and rest from work.

That question also underneath: the meaning
in Eliot of fire burning roses.
You never understood it, and
in high school lit your mother's garden,
hoping you would see it there, and know.

Forrest Hamer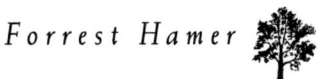

You didn't,
          and you burned your poems up,
setting out to make yourself less
violent and troubled. This worked,
you thought; except: the fury left
so spitefully it left you with no hope.
And here you are years later,
on the weekends, still sure the answer
is what you need to know to slow
things down and breathe through smoke.
You wonder if your violence has waited,
if it might come out here and settle.
Maybe you could live easily with fires,
grow things, let fire clear away
what strangles the merely unseen.

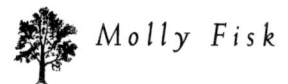 *Molly Fisk*

Angkor Wat

The idea is to build in your own heart a temple,
and worship with whatever is at hand:

one of a pair of yellow leather gloves
an elderly admirer gave you—his eyes wishing

you were 40 instead of 17—that long ago slipped
between cushions of a velvet chair. Or the suddenly-acquired sound

coming from your Volkswagen's lefthand, backseat speaker,
accompanying everything, happy cicada,

louder as the wires slowly pull and fray.
Everything you've lost is a prayer: bullfrog earrings, lovers,

the E above high C which now your voice only half-remembers
reaching clearly in the seventh grade,

and the iridescent hours that shimmer between time zones
on a flight from Singapore, catching the last of the orange sun,

in your lap: sun-colored stamen of the airline's complimentary orchid,
echo of ten thousand marigolds

at the feet of the Buddhas in Angkor Wat.
Years later you'll smile,

walking alone through a city park anywhere,
recognizing marigolds, yellow gloves.

Dan Bellm

Lament

for my father

There should be more empty space on the paper

there should be more empty space / than there was / before I wrote on it

I should clear the words away / to make space for the words unsaid / the words set aside / the words forgotten

I should leave the paper whiter than it was

I should make more room between the lines / for the intervals between words that last years / the indentations / the foreshortenings / the cropped borders

it should be plain what could have been written but was not / for loss of time / for theft of life

there should be fewer words now / for the sake of the one who has died / without a word / the way a gate shuts / the way time disappears / into heaven

there should be more silence for him / the one taught to ask less / told to wait without hope / left to comfort himself / who decided to tell no one / decided again every day / to tell no one

there should be more empty space on the paper / for the blessing choked back / for good

there should be a blinding darkness

a terrible / soundless / whirlwind / erasing

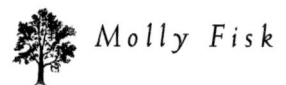 Molly Fisk

On the disinclination to scream

If I had been a ten year old stranger
and you had tripped me in a dark alley, say,
downtown, instead of our mutual living room
I'm sure I would have screamed.

If, in the alley, you had straddled me as fast—
your knees clamping my elbows into asphalt,
not the blue Chinese dragons
of our living room rug,
I might have been quiet there, too.

When you opened my mouth
with your heavy flat thumbs,
filled it with pain and flesh—
I would have choked in the alley,
as anyone would choke.

But if you had groaned then, and stood up,
walked away from the dark street
leaving me to vomit and shake alone,
I might have been saved.

Molly Fisk

I could describe you to policemen.
Perhaps their composite would match your photo
in the Harvard Reunion guide.
Your fingerprints, lifted from the collar of my dress,
might be found in Coast Guard files.

If they never found you and there was no trial
I could have gone home to people who loved me:
horrified, enraged, they would plot revenge
and rock me to sleep in soft arms.

I would have been frightened, maybe forever,
of alleys, strange men, and the dark—
but encouraged by the world, who would hate you on my behalf.
I would have been as safe as a ten year old can be.

Instead, I rose quietly from the Chinese rug
and went upstairs to wash.
No sound escaped me.
I couldn't afford to throw up,
and it wasn't the first time.

 Forrest Hamer

Invitation

I'd been doing so well: making conversation
at dinner parties, not being awkward.

But last Sunday, the blackberries were bleeding
in a cream-colored bowl, and I said something

about how picking through bramble to get juicy ones
left my hands kind of bloody when I was a kid,

and how blackberries taste mixed with blood.
Well, I could see frowns pricking polite smiles

—I wasn't fooled for a second—and when someone
changed the subject, and someone else moved away,

I was convinced coming had been a mistake. I should have
stayed at home, written a dinner party poem

where blackberries bleed without upsetting the host
and all of the guests lick their fingers.

Molly Fisk

The language

As a child in California I did not learn Spanish
like everyone else, the practical language.
In college I studied Norwegian, carefully placing
the l's out on the end of my tongue,
letting my hesitant breath swirl around them.

> l as in *melk* (milk), *flink* (clever)
> l as in *velkommen til Norge*

Whenever I could, I turned north—
toward the cool blue eyes and red beards,
the wooden ships and churches, reindeer,
cloudberries, snow.

> *reinsdyr, moltebaer, snø.*

What is the longing for all light? For none?
Like every heroine, I wanted to understand my life.

Whether or not you believe in coincidence,
and whether or not you like it, the word *sex*
in Norwegian still means six.

Molly Fisk

If everything is a sexual metaphor,
and if the Vikings populated two continents
by raping the native women, and if my father,
whom I still love, sailed to Norway
and brought me back a patterned sweater
before I was even born, if he was the one
who wandered into the wrong rooms at night,
where the inhabitants could not protest
because they didn't speak the language,
then why would I try to learn Spanish?

Dan Bellm

The peacemaker

I am traveling through ruined villages in an official delegation, and my job is to convince the people here to trust in us, that we will rebuild everything in time. But there are no actual encounters with people, only a landscape of enclosed places, bends in the road bordered by tall poplars, city stairways with no buildings beside them scaling dark hillsides under a closely hovering sky. Nor is anyone with me. Though I am part of a mission sent to speak to people who have suffered a war I find I am alone. I take this to mean that we will not be believed. The fields that were towns are flowering through the last of the snow, they are so beautifully green and peaceful, but I am required to understand they are utterly destroyed, I am required not to believe what I see. I find a building to live in, and once the rooms are emptied and the windows opened and new paint laid on and dried I want to put nothing back inside it, preferring blankness and discomfort, preferring to live someplace that will not be home, like a man who works every day and saves nothing of his work.

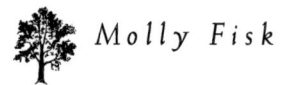

Molly Fisk

Prayer for Joe's Taco Lounge, Mill Valley

Fig-sized red and orange all-year Christmas bulbs
splash their holy light on the plastic-coated tablecloths
and glint against the bottled throats of every brand

of hot sauce—El Yucateco, Tapatio, Dona Maria's
Mole, singing their fiery songs on a shelf that lines the room,
nestled among a hundred ceramic Madonnas—

Tamazula, Cholula and Crystal beside the beatific
faces of the Mother of us all—and still lives of hard
plastic fruit not invented in this country, not even

in the Forties, and so many crosses, empty and occupied,
paintings of Jesus and the Lord. Oh, Bufalo,
Valentina, Tabasco, Habañero, guard the bas-relief

bull's head glowering out of its red velvet frame, bless
the photograph of somebody's mother, and the bluefin
tuna leaping on the wall, river of traffic flowing

past the plate glass, sanctify each hot tortilla,
each yellow plastic basket lined with greasy paper,
watch over the customers tonight as they bend

Molly Fisk

their heads to quesadillas and burritos, Del Fuerte,
if you are listening, carry us safely into tomorrow,
we will praise you by the artificial light of every

electrified tabletop candle, Oh gods of the spoon-shaped,
the smooth-skinned, searing chiles, comfort us—
keep us warm.

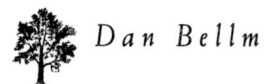 Dan Bellm

The last hour of the night

A boy wakes up before dawn
and pulls on his clothes from the chair,
gets up and walks downstairs and sits
by the window looking into
the dark. The little furnace
rattles and ticks above
the rush of flame
like matter and spirit. Light drops of rain
touch the glass. Outside in empty space,
reflected from the wall, Jesus
the protector and accuser
discloses his pierced heart.
There is a lighter darkness in the east,
a cluster of street lamps on the dark hill
in the west. The houses are rose-white,
each one a silhouette emerging into the day
alone. *I will go to the altar of God,*
to God who gives joy
to my youth. Then his mother is in the room,
he opens the door to the cold
and his clothes comfort his quivering skin,
he mouths the responses as they walk to church
without talking. *Introibo ad altare dei,*
ad deum qui laetificat

Dan Bellm

juventutem meam. He is afraid of making a mistake again,
sounding the chime at the wrong moment,
spilling the water as the priest
washes his hands for the holy rite
and chants the blessing down at him
with a look of blame. His mother
will console him later with a prayer, lighting a candle
at the Blessed Mother's altar.
But he leaves her at the side entrance
and the heavy door opens, and to the solitary man
looking up from his breviary in the darkly lit room
he whispers a *good morning Father*
that can't be heard. He counts out
the wafers of bread for the tabernacle,
prepares the water and wine,
puts on the alb and surplice and the pinching
collar. The wood and stone of the sacristy
are suffused with incense, the hoarded piety
of many cold mornings. It is the hour
before day has begun and wrongs are committed,
the hour of forgiveness. This darkness
must be the presence of God.

 Forrest Hamer

The calling

Text: A slave ship sinks in the Atlantic, 1749.

There must have been a great noise: the drumming and slap
of limbs against wood, ankles fit slack in shackles.

Children, there must have been a trembling violence,
bodies once more roused from a lumber of days, drunk
from the odor of shit and stilled in middle dance.

And, yes, there were terrible voices, the holler
wresting itself out, shouts silencing what babies
would tell, silencing even the goodness of God.

Don't you know there was a joy? that revenge came down
upon the men who chained them, who chained and locked them,
who would not look at them closely, not in the eyes;
that revenge had come from the body's dark water
to claim them all, even those who rendered feeling,
who swallowed and swallowed, swallowed deeply, then died.

And there must have been a moaning song that the land
heard about the deep grief of ocean, coward sky,
the brashness of resisting winds. Quiet
moves us to the edge of land and we lay ourselves
on it to listen; or, we lay ourselves inside.

Forrest Hamer

2.

    Aside from spirits, I was alone there,
and after I had cut the grass, put the mower back in the car,
      I lingered at my grandparents' graves.

    The sun settled while the air cooled itself off,
and dark trailed the oldest parts of the cemetery
      in full skirts. As I heard her slowly approach,

I imagined a hand come through the ground
as if the ground were as weightless as water,
and the hand calmly closed itself at my ankle,

my Mama Emma asking, *Stay, son*
      even though I could leave if I would
my Papa Willie said, *Yes. Stay, son*

      I was soon going North
to college, I told them; I was excited. I talked
about Mom becoming saved, Dad retiring from the Army,

my sister and the boy she secretly loved, my brother and how mean
      we were to each other without meaning to be,
         my dead brother whose grave no one had visited much.

And I told them what I had not been wanting to tell them—
that I had not been called to preach.

 Forrest Hamer

    I admitted I was feeling relieved, no longer worried

      about ignoring an unmistakable voice,
daring then to live in defiance of a terrible holy command
      to surrender and surrender again.

The dark stopped and nothing else moved,
      not even the waters of the ear, not even the heart.
      And when my grandparents finally spoke,

      they spoke with voices I have not yet recognized,
      reminded me to pray and to be good
      to people and to come back and sit with them at dusk.

      The dark moved on again, and clouds watched
me leave, the whole night smelling
suddenly of the saltwater roaring in my nose.

3.

A story my grandfather used to love
to tell had to do with his own baptism.
The preacher walked him into the muddy Neuse River
and they stood in there for a moment,
both of them dressed in white, both of them light.
And as my grandfather, a boy, really,
folded his arms across his chest—the way

Forrest Hamer

dead people sometimes do—the church members sang
Just As I Am. When the preacher embraced him,
and my grandfather began to fall
easily into deepness, a snake swam near enough
for them both to see. My grandfather threw
himself out of the preacher's arms, ran to land,
and the chuckling preacher called him back, for
he had seen many snakes in that river
and this serpent was not one to fear.

In the swimming pool, I am chuckling at my fear
of snakes in the pool. I hate the term Dead Man's Float,
but trust the teacher when he says I will
later feel calm and forget what I am
doing. What am doing is what I have tried
to learn twice before—how to breathe underwater,
how to trust that water entering my one good ear
will leave again, how to let water embrace
my body into descent. At the moment,
it is hardest to let my hips dance in that deep
space; the teacher has told us that men's trunks sink
our legs below the surface of water,
and this seems easily like sex. Yet,
the serpent waiting low in that water
is probably unconcerned with sin.
What is really making me feel naked in this class
is the presence of another black man.

 Forrest Hamer

4.

....and they saw not their father's nakedness
                              —Genesis 9:23

They walk in backwards.
They cover Noah.

Ham tries to forget what he has seen.
He tries to forget

that his father has only a man's body
His father is no God

Ham tries to forget the bending, the scars, the whiting hair

Ham tries to forget the penis, its tender shape

He tries to forget the shoulders gone round, the dragging chest

To forget breath, the craven let breath

And Ham tries to forget a prophecy
of his own short life which is now shorter than before
because his own body sometimes bends

voices beckoning

Dan Bellm

Illinois River

An island of white oak and red oak, cottonwood and red bud, a barge at
    Utica passing through the locks,

the petroleum and LP trucks warming up in the lot of the farm service
    bureau, the drivers blowing into their hands and pulling on
    gloves for the day's work,

a tarpaper house on stilts over the floodplain, a chimney covered with
    vines, a line of cypresses leaning to the river, a girl riding her
    bike with training wheels down the field of grass,

a tilting white cottage under the sandstone bluffs, a haymow, a hog pen,
    a swingset, a satellite dish,

prefab aluminum granaries, plastic lawn deer, cornflowers, bees and
    horseflies in the roadside grass and bickering starlings, three
    pickups crossing the ferry at Kampsville, the rural electrification
    plant,

water sprayed into a field from a soaker hose unwound from a heavy
    spool,

herbicide sprayed from a tank under the air-conditioned tractor and
    accumulating in the black soil, turning up years later in the
    drinking water at the bottom of the page in a newspaper report,

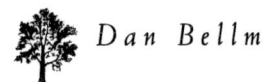 Dan Bellm

a boy and his father on their knees working in dirt, turning plowed-
       under scrub to grass and shrubbery with little patterns of gravel
       and stepping-stones, clearing away the pungent weeds that
       green the skin,

a freshly dug well, the raised welt from the backhoe running in a line all
       the way to the house and a man looking at his work, mud up
       both arms to the shoulder,

a red-tailed hawk, a turkey vulture, the gray feathers fluttering and
       parting on an owl's throat, the bird cooling itself in the midday
       heat,

a boarded-up gas station and machine shop, a rusted two-wheel oil tank
       leaning on its handle under the maple tree, two mobile homes
       and a tractor in front of a sagging, windowless farmhouse at
       Pearl,

black bears and wolves gone from this country like the Kickapoo, the
       Illinois, the Fox,

a hulking farm dog barking at the road long after the car has passed,

a quarry of lime and red rock, a road crew leaning at a steamroller to
       smoke,

Dan Bellm

the heat pausing, the air moist and sweet, the heavens pulling in a long
    breath and cutting loose a clattering downpour over and done in
    ten minutes then hauling back the sun, so that the fields steam
    again and the soaked trees sweat,

the county courthouse with a clock for each direction on the
    skullcapped square tower, the brick homes and clapboards
    through town along Route 4 with stone-pillared wraparound
    porches, the finest mansion in town a funeral home,

cousins playing catch at the family reunion while they wait for the
    birthday cake, the youngest baby standing himself up on
    unsteady feet on the blanket spread out in the shade, patting the
    trunk of the sycamore,

a man in Schuyler County estranged from his wife who takes his boys
    aged two and four out in the car and shoots them in the head by
    the side of the road near Rushville, then shoots himself, the
    younger boy safely strapped into his car seat in the back,

an auto graveyard, a Meadow Gold Dairy truck upended without
    wheels, a gravel pit, two wagon wheels at a driveway dotted
    with reflector caps,

a birdhouse in the shape of a riverboat, paper trash smoking in a burn
    barrel, a brown-spotted coyote crossing the road, a one-lane
    bridge,

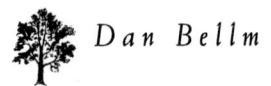 *Dan Bellm*

    generations of washing machines and oil cans, mower blades and truck parts, piled in a neat square patch in back of the house and overgrown with tall grass,

    Hardee's and Taco Bell and Target and Wal-Mart, all new, floating in acres of parking under the tall lights, the edge of the city spreading into the flat darkness,

    a grassland scraped flat by a thousand years of ice, teeming, passive, forgiving, unprepared, the richest soil on earth,

    a drawbridge missing green paint in the section that had to be repaired, and a farmer sitting in his truck waiting to cross, patiently reading the death notices in the county paper, one hand on the wheel,

    a yellow band of wheat, and bands of darker and lighter green in the bean and corn fields down the slope to the river, and the sun falling open over the riverbank woods.

Molly Fisk

"the names of streets instead of streets..."

When, in Oslo, I skied down the main street, pushing off
against the white rim of the world, gliding past
the train station and the famous nude statues, I spoke
a language of my own, the *gammelnorsk* Margit taught me
from before the war mixed with a little *grisprat*
I learned in Vågå. I got along, but there is something
about living in a language you don't own that teaches you
the first steps of dying. Without the slanted American puns
and dumb jokes, nothing special, just what anyone
would know, I was diminished, I was not myself,
and I carry it, mixed in with cold nights and lilting vowels:
chilled breath from the other side of heaven.

I will always belong to the Spanish names of California,
but I liked the pushed-forwardness of that arctic speech,
the precarious ring of those ls against the top of my teeth,
suspended like icicles: *Jeg elsker deg, du elsker meg,
velkommen til Norge*, and the way you have to almost smile
to get the *e* right, hardly opening your mouth, since at that latitude
everything, even the language, is based on trying to stay warm.
I was someone in Norwegian but I don't know who—
and when a Viking wrapped me in his sweatered arms
against the wind and called my name into the northern sky,
I couldn't help it—under my breath I said San Francisco,
I said Divisadero, I said Anza, Balboa, Cabrillo.

 Forrest Hamer

Moving on

        1.

When my father finally spoke to me
about war, he didn't mention Viet Nam
but a bone-chill Korea, cleaved into before
I was born. And he told me a white man
saved his life there, the white man

his friend, another Southerner
away from home for the first time.
Billy McGee saw the land mine my father
almost tripped, and he moved him
out of the way. When McGee moved on,

        2.

stateside, my father said he missed him
openly and for days, until another
white soldier, also a Southerner,
told my father what the other whites knew,
that McGee belonged to the Klan

Forrest Hamer

back in South Carolina, and he'd boasted
he was even one of their leaders.
My father's sadness ended quick, he said,
and he never write the letters he had
promised, never heard again from McGee.

      3.

My father hasn't told me I could tell this.
He didn't say I could show the naive love
he can have for men, how ashamed a man
who is also a black man can be when
a white man saves his life. But when he says

he doesn't care whatever happened
to Billy McGee, he hasn't told me
not to wonder whether people do move
each other in the end, or if saving
someone's story is the same as saving life.

      4.

During my father's second Viet Nam tour,
something between us changed—he came back startled
and quiet. And I began demanding
he let me wear my hair long and in braids.
We seemed to find no more to say, so

 Forrest Hamer

I plotted to leave my father's house.
Once every few months, after some fight,
I asked him what had happened over there.
There was nothing to tell me, he said:
he came home, a lot of others didn't.

        5.

Leaving a father's house is never as easy
as moving away. For a long time, sometimes
always, one of them, the father, the child,
wishes away ever having loved the other,
and the other resents being loved this way.

When I became grown, and my father began ending
the rest of his life, he finally told me
about war and the man there who saved him.
My father told me that was the blessing
I'd wanted. He asked me to give him mine.

Molly Fisk

Hunter's moon

Early December, dusk, and the sky
slips down the rungs of its blue ladder
into indigo. A late-quarter moon hangs
in the air above the ridge like a broken plate
and shines on us all, on the new deputy
almost asleep in his four-by-four,
lulled by the crackling song of the dispatcher,
on the bartender, slowly wiping a glass
and racking it, one eye checking the game.
It shines down on the fox's red and grey life,
as he stills, a shadow beside someone's gate,
listening to winter. Its pale gaze caresses
the lovers, curled together under a quilt,
dreaming alone, and shines on the scattered
ashes of terrible fires, on the owl's black flight,
on the whelks, on the murmuring kelp,
on the whale that washed up six weeks ago
at the base of the dunes, and it shines
on the backhoe that buried her.

 Forrest Hamer

Arrival, the city of Bethames

And in the middle time of traveling,
he came upon a man doubting
and he lingered with him for several nights,
feeding on rain. He found himself
sinking into underearth, his body
eager to let go. Sliding through slick,
he began to see through the dark.
I shall lose my way, he thought,
journey no longer worth minding,
but the rain seeping easy into his mouth
turned a furious ocean.
He would dream only of crossing it.

Dan Bellm

Nashvillanelle

I've told you everything I have to say;
Now go. You're like that truck-stop country song,
How can I miss you, when you won't go away?—

The one that, wishing you'd laugh, I used to play
On air guitar the summer we came unstrung.
I've told you everything I have to say:

Lie down and rest, Dad. Deny it as you may,
You're dead, you know. I saw you die. So long.
How can I miss you when you won't go away?

I place such trust that, placed the proper way,
The right words make things right, but am I wrong?
I've told you everything I have to say,

Expecting what? A way with words to outweigh
Your way with silence, that's so final and so strong?
How can I miss you when you won't go away?

You linger as if death's cast you astray,
The same as life. Is there no place you belong?
I've told you everything I have to say.
How can I miss you, when you won't go away?

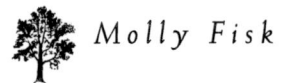 *Molly Fisk*

Surface tension

It's like the instant your canoe tilts
over the edge, the way it hangs
for a beat or two, reluctant to leave
calm water, then shoots forward
to meet the rapid; the second
after they've fired the rocket into the air
on the 4th of July and it hasn't opened yet,
it's just one dot of light, you hold
the silvery shower of stars behind your eyes,
remembering last year, childhood,
just for a second, until it blooms;
like the moment when, tangled
in a half-lit room, he comes
and you're watching him, the hard breath,
his back arched against your palms,
the way he cannot stop his legs from shaking.

Forrest Hamer

Getting happy

When the men got happy in church,
        they shouted and jumped straight up.

But the women's trances
        made them dance with moaning; so,

I dreaded Rev. Johnson's sermons
        near their end, hated the trouble

he was causing inside
        the souls of women sweating

and beginning to breathe fast.
        One day, I worried, my mother

would let go and lose herself
        to him, become as giddy

as when my father was coming home
        on leave. Just as silly.

Yet, when it finally happened,
        I felt only left behind.

 Forrest Hamer

Years later, another first time,
        I heard my moan echo inside

a girl's ear and recognized
        how woeful pleasure feels.

I then began to wonder
        if there weren't some joy still

to give in to, make me shout
        not as men do, but as a woman.

It troubles me.
        I do not have a woman's body

but fear that moaning will betray
        this want in me, or another

to be like a woman. Mostly,
        I fear that moaning will uncover

the love for my mother that is still
        so deep that I want little more

than to be with her as closely as I can.

Dan Bellm

Boy wearing a dress

On the way home he asks me, *If we cut off our
penises then we'd be girls wouldn't we Dad,*
my little boy in cowboy boots and a long black dress
walking home from Castro Street playing
blue fairy and wicked stepsister and lost princess as he
walks, the people and store windows whirling by

as he twirls only figures in fairy stories he knows by
heart, though what he doesn't see yet is that our
neighborhood's a kind of fairyland for real—still, I hope no one heard him
ask me that, and hope my Dad
who is dead hasn't heard, who would never have let me play
boy and girl with this frightening freedom, dressing

up in public or alone in a four-dollar thrift-store dress
we bought because he asked for one. A drunk careening by
asks, *Why who are you some kind of superhero, son,* and from a display
window video porno stars sweating under harsh light smirk in our
faces—*I don't have to tell them who I am now do I Dad*—
No it's a dress, the guy's friend says, *I've seen him*

*around before, that boy's always in costume, he
must be a little fag.* Ken dolls in white satin dresses
and angel wings and hairless Barbies done up as leather Dads

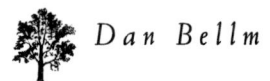 *Dan Bellm*

are climbing a Christmas tree inside the card shop by
the pizza store, some queen's fantasy scenario of what our
mothers and fathers should have let us play

back where we come from, but my little boy likes to play
the girl parts of stories for reasons of his own, he
likes their speeches and their dresses and shoes, we tell ourselves
it's harmless, wanting to wear a dress,
harmless as my nervous laughter to passersby
and what do I apologize to them for, Dad—

When I was a child I wanted to wear my Dad's
work shirts, I liked the smell of his Army uniform, I didn't play
girl games, don't look at me. My little boy is getting distracted by
the dildoes at the sex shop I try to hustle him past. Soon enough he'll
learn to leave his dress at home, will hear somewhere that a boy in a dress
cannot be beautiful. Once inside our

house he undresses by the mirror to be naked under the dress,
and lifts it up to display what most of us keep inside our
pants, and he asks me, a little afraid for the answer, *Am I beautiful, Dad*—

Molly Fisk

The Dry Tortugas

They were building a house in the Dry Tortugas,
less for the solitude there than the open eyes
of a swallowtailed hummingbird they had seen once
on a fishing trip—the early Fifties, he reeling in
an oversized yellowfin, Humphrey Bogart
facing the wind, one foot on the rail in *To Have and Have Not*,
she whistling the stuttered call of the Amazonian kingfisher,
and singing in Spanish to flocks of Bonaparte gulls.
It comes to nothing in the end, though the land
is paced off and measured and two palms felled
to expand the view, a road graded the requisite mile,
and some of their friends fly down from New York
to surprise them, circle the islands all morning, gleeful and chic
in their 4-seater Cessna (he's something exalted at Chase),
and later the bottles of Myer's and Appleton Gold sweat
dark rings on the terrace flagstones, and someone's pink
lipstick makes delicate kissprints along the rim of her glass.
No one has told me what happened—his heart
attack in Guatemala, her premonition about the wide
and empty view, or the world swinging in
with its usual brazen distractions—but they framed
the architect's plans of the house, and this
is what I inherit, a rendering in colored pencil:
what they were dreaming before I was born.

About the Poets

Dan Bellm lives in San Francisco. His collection of poems, *One Hand on the Wheel*, will launch the new California Poetry Series from Roundhouse Press, Berkeley, in April 1999. A second collection, *Buried Treasure*, which won the 1995 Alice Fay DiCastagnola Award from the Poetry Society of America, will be published in September 1999 by Cleveland State University Press as winner of its annual Poetry Center Prize. He received a 1997 poetry fellowship from the California Arts Council.

Molly Fisk lives in Nevada City, California, where she works as the Executive Director of Literature Alive!, editor of *The Healing Woman*, and poetry editor of *Estero: A West Marin Quarterly*. Her hand letterpress chapbook *Salt Water Poems* came out in 1994, as well as *Surrender*, a spoken word audiotape. She teaches with U.C. Davis Extension and California Poets in the Schools, and has received poetry fellowships from the California Arts Council (1997) and the Marin County Arts Council (1995).

Forrest Hamer lives in Oakland. His book of poems, *Call & Response*, published by Alice James Books in 1995, won the Beatrice Hawley Award and was a semi-finalist for the Poet's Prize. He is a psychologist, a candidate psychoanalyst, and a lecturer at the University of California at Berkeley.